EARLY INTERMEDIATE

TAKE A BOW!

8 SPARKLING PIANO SOLOS

GREAT RECITAL PIECES!

BOOK 4

BY CAROLYN

ISBN 978-1-61774-269-9

WILLIS MUSIC

EXCLUSIVELY DISTRIBUTED BY

**HAL•LEONARD®
CORPORATION**

7777 W. BLUEMOUND RD. P.O. BOX 13819 MILWAUKEE, WI 53213

© 2011 by The Willis Music Co.
International Copyright Secured   All Rights Reserved

For all works contained herein:
Unauthorized copying, arranging, adapting, recording, Internet posting, public performance,
or other distribution of the printed music in this publication is an infringement of copyright.
Infringers are liable under the law.

Visit Hal Leonard Online at
www.halleonard.com

FROM THE COMPOSER

Recital time should be a happy time! I believe that the recital solo should be carefully chosen to give each student the best chance for success in front of an unfamiliar audience. It is my hope that students will master the carefully selected solos in this book so that a winning performance takes place.

In this book you'll find that I am often inspired and captivated with the illusion of flight and floating—"The Dancing Butterfly," "Flying Away" and "Soft Ocean Breeze." I wrote "Alaskan Majesty" after witnessing the beauty and grandeur of the glaciers on a wonderful trip to the state. It allows the student to practice and play deep, sinking chords, and finishes with a satisfying grandioso ending. And I hope that the rhythmic "Catwalk Strut" elicits a smart, sassy performance!

My wish is that these pieces will entertain as well as motivate students of any age.

Please enjoy!

Carolyn Miller

ABOUT THE COMPOSER

Carolyn Miller's teaching and composing career spans over 40 prolific years. She graduated with honors from the College Conservatory of Music at the University of Cincinnati with a degree in music education, and later earned a masters degree in elementary education from Xavier University. Carolyn regularly presents workshops throughout the United States and is a frequent adjudicator at festivals and competitions. Although she recently retired from the Cincinnati public school system, she continues to maintain her own private studio.

Carolyn's music emphasizes essential technical skills, is remarkably fun to play, and appeals to both children and adults. Well-known television personality Regis Philbin performed her pieces "Rolling River" and "Fireflies" in 1992 and 1993 on national television. Carolyn's compositions appear frequently on state contest lists, including the NFMC Festivals Bulletin. She is listed in the *Who's Who in America* and *Who's Who of American Women*.

In her spare time Carolyn directs the Northminster Presbyterian Church Choir in Cincinnati, Ohio and enjoys spending time with her family, especially her seven grandchildren.

Catwalk Strut

Carolyn Miller

© 2011 by The Willis Music Co.
International Copyright Secured   All Rights Reserved

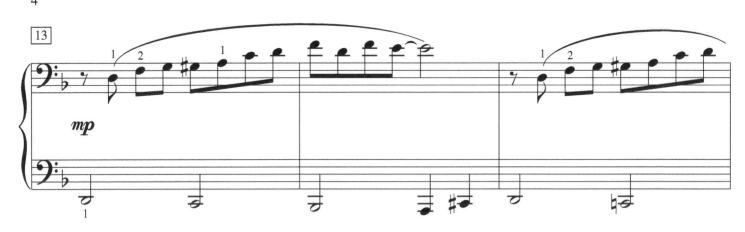

Soft Ocean Breeze

Carolyn Miller

Andante, with much rubato

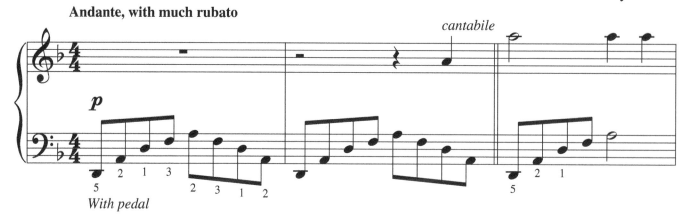

© 2011 by The Willis Music Co.
International Copyright Secured   All Rights Reserved

The Dancing Butterfly

Carolyn Miller

© 2000 by The Willis Music Co.
International Copyright Secured   All Rights Reserved

Etude in C Minor
(Alla Tarantella)

Carolyn Miller
Revised by David Engle

© 1994 by The Willis Music Co.
International Copyright Secured   All Rights Reserved

Scaling the Heights

Carolyn Miller

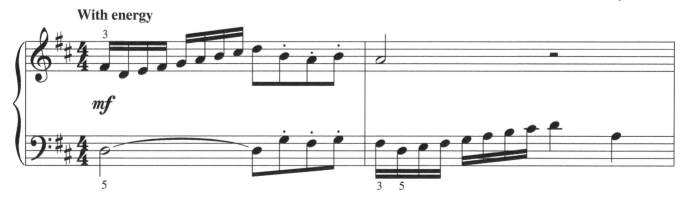

© 1997 by The Willis Music Co.
International Copyright Secured   All Rights Reserved

Alaskan Majesty

Carolyn Miller

© 1999 by The Willis Music Co.
International Copyright Secured   All Rights Reserved

Flying Away

Carolyn Miller

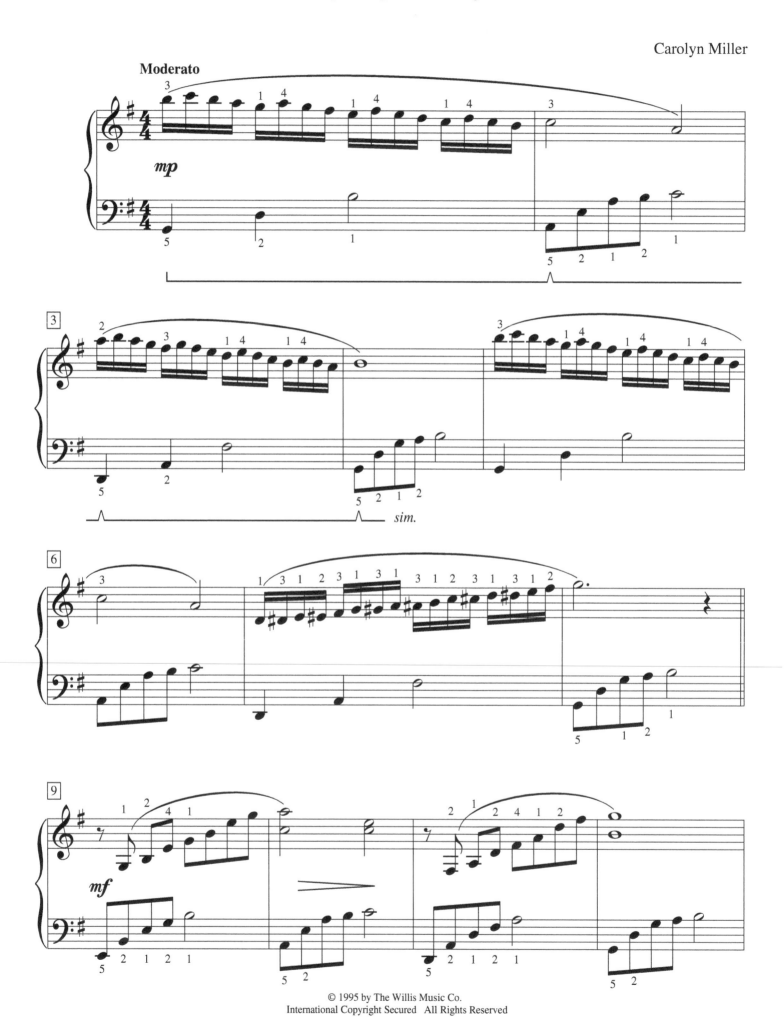

© 1995 by The Willis Music Co.
International Copyright Secured   All Rights Reserved

Chromatic Adventure

Carolyn Miller

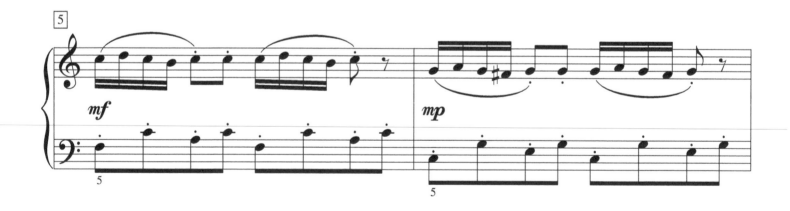

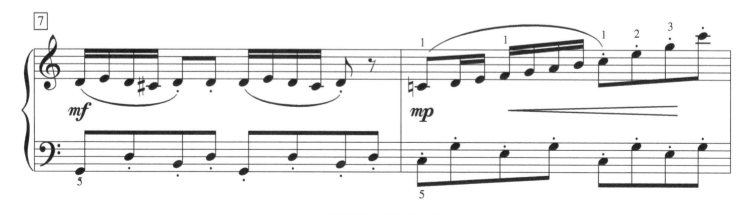

© 2011 by The Willis Music Co.
International Copyright Secured   All Rights Reserved